POSSIBILITY

Our Advent Journey with the Prophet, Priest, Pastor, & Poet

BRUCE REYES-CHOW

chalice
PRESS

Print: 9780827231979

EPUB: 9780827231986

EPDF: 9780827231993

ChalicePress.com

Printed in the United States of America

Contents

Welcome

Advent signals the beginning of a new church year. And yet, in 2025-2026, the world is living in a constate state of political and social turmoil. Solutions seem few and far between. One cathartic and healing act of resistance could be to view our current time through the lens of "possibility." In this daily devotional, I invite you to embrace and embody possibility, that is possibility grounded in the fullness of Jesus. Not only the Jesus we prefer to see (the One who often looks a lot like us), but the Christ in His fullness: Prophet, Priest, Pastor, and Poet.

The fourfold Jesus is more fully fleshed out in the book *Prophets, Priests, Pastors, & Poets: Being and Becoming the Resurrected Christ* (Chalice Media, 2026) and is the foundation and inspiration for *Possibility*.

PROPHET: A table-turning activist, political troublemaker, and cultural provocateur who with righteous indignation, passion, and courage challenges the world to align with God's hopes.

PRIEST: A going-off-to-pray, miracle-worker spiritual teacher who curates holy spaces, nurtures spiritual discipline, tends our histories, and invites us into ritual as ways to connect to God.

PASTOR: A "giving the benefit of the doubt" convener of relationships, instigator of belonging, and unapologetic bridge builder who yearns for us to cross cultural, economic, and theological divides as a way to know the expansiveness of God's creation.

POET: A "more questions than answers" sculptor of words, ideas, and actions and the one who pries open the human imagination in order to see the possibilities that God has for the world.

Each day includes:

A biblical text using the Common English Bible with non-gendered language for God.	A brief reflection from my life observing the world through the lens of Gen X, California pastor, parent, person of color, and lover of all food.

A question for thought that can be used by individuals or groups.	A brief prayer to ground your day.

Each of the Sundays in Advent focuses on one of the four natures of Christ — Hope & The Prophet, Peace & The Priest, Joy & The Pastor, Love & The Poet — and includes an Advent candle lighting litany and a preaching prompt.

Advent Candle Lighting Litany	Preaching Prompt

Thank you for allowing me to join you during this Advent season. I hope your heart, mind, and spirit, and the possibilities that Christ offers to the world, will be made known to you every day.

Peace to you,

Bruce

The First Sunday in Advent

DAY 1: The First Sunday in Advent

HOPE & THE PROPHET

Watch out! Stay alert! You don't know when the time is coming. — **Mark 13:33 (CEB)**

I love Advent. While you will find no elves on shelves or pumpkin-spiced items in my orbit, you will find a stash of cheesy holiday rom-coms, holiday playlists, and solid ugly sweaters. Most exciting, however, is the anticipation of what is to come, the liturgical invitation to enter into a season of anticipation and the disruption of the world's suffering.

We begin with the Prophet Jesus' notion of hope and the disruptive possibility of a healed world beyond the pain that it bears today. This promise reminds me that despair does not have the last word. It nudges me to get off my duff and live in the world as if the coming of the little baby Jesus matters.

So as you step into Advent for the first or the fiftieth time, let's prepare for the disruption of despair by making room for hope and embracing the possibilities Christ offers.

What situations in the world most need to be disrupted by the hope that Christ offers? How might you go out and be that hope?

Advent Candle Lighting Litany

One: Immanuel, "God with us," as we light the candle of hope, we remember that Jesus comes into the world as the Prophet with us.

ALL: God, you enter the world to disrupt the hold that despair has on it and to remind us that hope will win this and every day.

One: So with courage, clarity, and conviction, we light the candle of HOPE.

Light the candle of hope.

One: Joining the prophets of the past and calling the prophets of the future...

ALL:...the prophets together say, AMEN.

Preaching Prompt: Be bold in naming the places in need of disruption (both within and outside the community) by what you believe God is calling the church to be and become.

*The lighting of the Advent wreath can be a lovely time to explore different expressions of the Advent season, so be courageous and creative. Lift up a variety of voices and life experiences. Try using different colored candles. My favorite is using a brown candle for Jesus on Christmas Eve. Or use the four-week season to experiment with something creative and colorful.

DAY 2

DISTRESS

There will be great suffering such as the world has never before seen and will never again see. — **Matthew 24:21 (CEB)**

Distress in the world, let us count the ways: racism, misogyny, climate crisis, gun violence, health care affordability, education accessibility, wealth disparity, police brutality, antisemitism, Islamophobia, xenophobia, homophobia, Christian nationalism, war, hunger, suffering on our screens, suffering in the shadows, and the general terribleness of the world. Sometimes, I just want to curl up in the comfortable cocoon of my privilege with a bag of chips and hide until it's safe to emerge.

Of course, we will all deal with these situations differently; sometimes we step back, sometimes we go rushing in, sometimes we go ourselves, and other times we support others. What the Poet Jesus challenges us to remember is that distress, no matter how hard, shall not have the last word and that there is the promise of something beyond what we can imagine. We know not the time or the tempo, but we do know it will come.

So, during this Advent, let's hold the distress tenderly when we need to or challenge it when it is called for. But let's never allow the distress to define us for eternity. Let's also remember amid temporary distress we have the promise of new life found in the one called Christ.

What situation in the world right now do you have the most difficult time seeing a way out of?

God with us –

We may not know how, when, or why

Even in our greatest distress.

Give us the courage to remember

That your promise of new life remains true.

– AMEN

DAY 3

EXPECTATIONS

All these people didn't receive what was promised, though they were given approval for their faith. God provided something better for us so they wouldn't be made perfect without us.
— Hebrews 11:39–40 (CEB)

Humanoids like control. Their need for control will be expressed differently from person to person, but even the most laid-back souls have an area of their lives where they must maintain control. This is not good or bad; it is simply a reality for most of us.

While planning is certainly helpful in most cases, it can also be limiting if we become too attached to a particular outcome. That is true, especially if we are unable to deal with alternative possibilities. The Poet Jesus does not encourage us to think more broadly just for the sake of being different. God may reveal before we make future plans. If we are unable to loosen our hold on our expectations, we might miss out on experiencing something greater than we had ever expected in the first place.

So yes, we must plan. Yes, we must have expectations, but we must hold them tenderly and make room for God to shape and form them into what God intends, not just what we want.

Name a time when you had decided on a plan but you believe God had a different one.

God with us –

We don't know what will happen,

but we yearn to know.

As we wait and wait and wait,

let us trust and trust and trust.

– AMEN

DAY 4

TRICKERY

False christs and false prophets will appear, and they will offer great signs and wonders in order to deceive, if possible, even those whom God has chosen. — **Matthew 24:24 (CEB)**

I have always found it easy to pick out the hucksters in the world. Mostly because they disagree with me; and, in my sophisticated mind, they are just dum-dum poopy-heads.

While I may not be wrong in my assessment about what snake oil they are selling, Priestly Jesus' encouragement to be self-reflective is, annoyingly, still there. In my case, that means remembering that there is a high probability that someone, somewhere, is thinking the exact same thing about what I offer to the world: "Man, that Bruce guy is a dum-dum poopy-head." Knowing that I could also be "that guy" does not stop me from striving for truth, but it does force me to judge with more humility and care.

So we must be wise this Advent. We seek the truth spoken into the world but know that just as we may reject another person's speaking as foolishness, someone else probably has the same thought about us.

Fair or not, how might people who disagree with you judge you?

God with us –

Grant us equal measures:

the courage to assume goodness

the wisdom to recognize deceit

and humility enough to know

when the real deceivers are us.

– AMEN

DAY 5

HEALING

The moon will shine like the sun, and the sunlight will be seven times brighter, like the light of seven full days, when God binds up the bruises of the people and heals the wounds inflicted.
— Isaiah 30:26 (NIV)

When I am hurting, I choose to believe that healing eventually will come: healing of my heart, healing of my body, or healing of my spirit. Do I know for a fact that I will be healed, or healed in the ways that I want? Nope—but I trust God anyway.

Choosing to believe in healing, especially in the midst of pain in body, mind, or spirit, is not easy, and often the healing does not happen the way I want. While healing can come in many ways, the Pastoral Jesus helps to create space for the complexity of healing to be made real through the experience of community.

This Advent, let's recommit to believing that, even in our deepest pains and wounds, we will, at some point and in some way, know God's healing and wholeness.

As much as you can, name the areas in your life and the world that are in the deepest need of healing.

God with us –

We do not always understand the depths

of our pain, struggle, and despair,

but when your healing is known

let us all receive it gladly.

– AMEN

DAY 6

COMFORT

Like a shepherd, God will tend the flock; they will gather lambs in their arms and lift them onto their lap. They will gently guide the nursing ewes. — **Isaiah 40:11 (CEB, non-gendered)**

Comforting others is tricky. Some people recoil from physical embraces, while others hungrily feed off of all hugs offered during times of turmoil. And still others either have a difficult time or are not in the space to receive comfort.

When offering comfort, we must ensure it is given in a way that the recipient can truly experience our good intentions. None of us comes to interactions as a blank slate. Our past pain impacts how we react to others' gestures. Everyone experiences healing differently, and what comforts one person may not work for another.

The Pastoral Jesus invites us into community in ways as diverse and expansive as the lives of those who need that comfort, so no matter how you extend a comforting hand or gesture to one in pain, let it be one that is caring and compassionate, all the while remembering that God promises to do the same.

Share a time when you have had to adjust the way that you have needed to offer comfort to someone because of something you learned about them or about yourself?

God with us –

With the empathetic warmth of a genuine embrace

when our bodies and souls are weary and hurting,

let your comfort be known, felt, and believed.

- AMEN

DAY 7

PURITY

God didn't call us to be immoral but to be dedicated to God
— 1 Thessalonians 4:7 (CEB, non-gendered)

The purity wars! Ugh.

Arguably, one of the worst, most dangerous manifestations of Christian practices is when Christians begin to litmus test one another: in politics, in culture, and, of course, in doctrine. We litmus test by how we vote on a particular issue, what we share or do not share on social media, or how we express a singular theological position.

Too many people claim that God loves everyone but still hold a rigid understanding of who is "in" and who is "out." We can each hold core beliefs. However, if we believe that our particular slice of the Christian pie determines what makes a true, pure, or right Christian, then we are playing God.

All aspects of Jesus are showing up for this one:

- the Prophet to disrupt litmus test Christianity
- the Priest to invite people into deeper discernment
- the Pastor to engage with the breadth of the human experience
- and the Poet to think more expansively about faith as a whole

So through it all, we can hold strong beliefs, but we must likewise also tend to our humble spirits. We are many wonderful things, but God we are not.

Are there any litmus tests, spoken or unspoken, in your community that need to be addressed?

God with us –

Beckon us to a life that is pure,

not purity built upon power and shame

but a purity that honors you

with love and liberation.

– AMEN

The Second Sunday in Advent

DAY 8: THE SECOND SUNDAY IN ADVENT

PEACE & THE PRIEST

Produce fruit that shows you have changed your hearts and lives. — **Matthew 3:8 (CEB)**

Sometimes when I look out at the world, it feels like conflict is winning. It would be easy to give up because our peacemaking work seems in vain. It is not. The Priestly Jesus reminds us that, in response to the peace Jesus offers us, we must be grounded in the peace we hope to see in the world. Too often, the world sees peace as an absence of conflict, violence, or anxiety. While these are noble hopes for the world, peace is much more than an absence of strife but rather a presence of justice.

We all know how to put on a brave face and look as if all is well, at least from the outside. But true peace understands that until we seek and know peace at the depths of our soul, we end up ignoring—even exacerbating—the spaces that need to know peace all around us.

For the world to know peace, we must commit to showing peace, to allowing peace to be woven in the cells of our body, and to living fully the peace we hope to see in the world.

Advent Candle Lighting Litany

One: Immanuel, "God with us," as we light the candle of peace, we remember that Jesus comes into the world as a Priest with us.

ALL: God, you enter the world and remind us that the strength of our faith is built upon the prayers of our ancestors, the richness of our traditions, and the curiosity of our minds.

One: So with curiosity, discipline, and ritual, we light the candle of PEACE.

Light the candle of peace.

One: Joining the priests of the past and calling the priests of the future...

ALL:...the priests of today together say, AMEN.

Preaching Prompt: Name the situations that are in need of peace, not just peace in a big picture sense, but in a way that challenges people of God to be enactors of peace in ways that are bold, courageous, and even risky.

DAY 9

HUMILITY

My siblings, I myself am convinced that you yourselves are full of goodness, filled with all knowledge, and are able to teach each other. — **Romans 15:14 (CEB, non-gendered)**

As the father of three children who have identified as female for most of their lives, it has become clear that the world finds ways to communicate the false narrative that to be female means to be weak and less than their male counterparts.

The constant barrage of these negative messages is insidious. And at the same time constant overwhelming praise is not always helpful. These two must be held in healthy tension. We must be careful in how we offer praise or critique, helping our offspring maintain a harmony between confidence and humility. Faithful self-reflection and discernment, both encouraging them in others and exercising them ourselves, are exactly what the Priestly Jesus invites us into. In the compliments and the critiques, we must embrace that which will help us grow into who God intends and let go of that which will tear us down.

Whether individuals, communities, or even societies are holding this tension between confidence and humility, constantly engaging in this work allows us to grow into who God intends us to be and become.

Share something about yourself that you are confident about, and something that you may not be so.

God with us –

We choose to believe

that we are your beloved:

capable, called, and created.

In this, let our calling be fueled by

confidence and not conceit.

– AMEN

DAY 10

WORDS

By your words you will be either judged innocent or condemned as guilty. — **Matthew 12:37 (CEB)**

The old saying goes, "Sticks and stones can break my bones, but words will never hurt me." As a defense mechanism, this can sometimes be helpful to remember—at least at a technical level.

That said, we also know that words can indeed cause harm to others. Charges of being "oversensitive" are often leveled at those who challenge language used to marginalize others or incite violence. And challenging others to be responsible for the impact and repercussions of how we use words is labelled as "politically correct." The Prophetic Jesus would challenge the idea that being empathetic towards others' feelings is a weakness. In fact, it is how God intends for humans to interact with one another.

Because I believe that the words we use matter, I, for one, will always err on the side of speaking words that do no harm at their worst and build up the other at their best. The words we use have an impact on people: both words of hate and words of kindness. I will always choose the latter.

How has your vocabulary changed over time because you understand the impact of words?

God with us –

Just as our hands can harm,

remind us of the pain

we can inflict with our words.

And let our words not hurt, but heal.

- AMEN

DAY 11

FORGETTING

But they fail to notice that, by God's word, heaven and earth were formed long ago out of water and by means of water.
— 2 Peter 3:5 (CEB)

I often have a hard time even remembering where I put my keys, so, trying to remember every lesson of hope that God has for me in the world is daunting.

In many aspects of our lives, the seductive nature of comfort and security can often lead us to forget that God is and was present then, now, and tomorrow.

Enter the Priestly Jesus, who calls us to remember to whom we belong, who has come before us, and what has been promised. We must not forget how God has acted in the world, over the generations and through our ancestors. We also must not forget how God has been active in our own lives and remember that God promises to remember us and always will.

In a world weighed down with so much social chaos, political turmoil, privilege, escapism, and personal pursuits, we can find ourselves confined in spaces of forgetfulness. Advent is simply a time when we can make disciplined attempts to remember that God has been and will be with us through it all.

Talk about an ancestor or saint who has impacted your faith.

God with us –

When we choose to forget you again,

remind us of your expanse,

your creation, and your power.

And let us embrace and remember it all.

– AMEN

DAY 12

POWER

God: who protects immigrants, who helps orphans and widows, but who makes the way of the wicked twist and turn!
— Psalm 146:9 (CEB, non-gendered)

Power—social, political, or relational—is not a bad thing in itself. Like any influence we hold, we can use it either to build up or to tear down.

Unfortunately, too often power is used to protect and build up what the powerful already possess: resources, political influence, and *more power*. When the powerful adopt a posture of self-preservation, exclusion, and destruction, it is the powerless who suffer: those in poverty, those without access to resources, and those who are on the outside looking in.

The Prophet Jesus shows up the most to challenge those in power, and because he did this, those in power killed him. It is that simple. Power that feeds on the pain and oppression of others will never tell a story of healing and liberation, so the Prophet Jesus challenges us to tell God's story for humanity.

To turn back the tide of oppressive use of power, a different story must be told: one of hospitality, generosity, and kindness. For when we challenge the triumphalism that we know currently is happening in the world, and even in our own country, we will enact the power that God has given to our care and for our use in the world today.

What are ways that you see power being used well today?

God with us –

When we behave as if You would

take the side of the wealthy and powerful,

remind us that the poor and oppressed

pay the price.

– AMEN

DAY 13

GENEROSITY

The crowds asked him, "What then should we do?" He answered, "Whoever has two shirts must share with the one who has none, and whoever has food must do the same." Even tax collectors came to be baptized. They said to him, "Teacher, what should we do?" He replied, "Collect no more than you are authorized to collect." Soldiers asked, "What about us? What should we do?" He answered, "Don't cheat or harass anyone, and be satisfied with your pay." — **Luke 3:10–14 (CEB)**

Whether sharing our favorite toys when young or sharing our financial resources as we age, sharing is hard. Always has been, and always will be. But to share with others what we need to sustain our own comfort and security is a loving, revolutionary act of faith.

One difficult aspect of sharing is that we trick ourselves into believing that we do not have enough to share. Scarcity thinking is insidious and causes us to hoard because we believe that we will never have enough. The Poet Jesus, in all that he does from every miracle and every healing, reminds us that scarcity is not where the people of the resurrection live. We live in the abundance of love that new life provides.

The fact is that for many of us, not only do we have enough, we have an abundance. And it is precisely in response to that abundance that we should share freely.

Where does your community have abundance, where sometimes it believes there is scarcity?

God with us –

When we grasp so tightly

to wealth born of the world

remind us of your abundant acts

and give us the courage to do likewise.

– AMEN

DAY 14

LIVING

Wherever the river flows, every living thing that moves will thrive. There will be great schools of fish, because when these waters enter the sea, it will be fresh. Wherever the river flows, everything will live. — **Ezekiel 47:9 (CEB)**

As resurrection people, we believe that death and despair will not have the final word. We say this—but honestly, sometimes with the amount of violence, sorrow, and suffering that bombards our senses every day, it is difficult to believe in our very being.

This is where the Priestly Jesus calls us into a ritual of thanksgiving, for in a world where destruction seems to rule the airwaves, it is crucial that we also name life-giving situations: the unexpected act of kindness by a stranger, hanging out with friends for no particular reason, or watching God show off with a gorgeous sunset. If we fail to see life around us while confronting death that tries to overcome us, we will become the people for whom hope and resurrection are reduced to intellectual whimsy.

In the face of death and despair, it is crucial to choose lives of hope. Life is not only possible but promised to us by God. While it is not always clear to see that, for the health of our spirits and the good of the world, I hope we will.

Name as a few places of life that you have noticed in the past week.

God with us –

Death and despair surround us.

You promise life and hope.

Let us choose this life.

Let us choose this hope.

Let us choose this faith.

– AMEN

The Third Sunday in Advent

DAY 15: THE THIRD SUNDAY IN ADVENT

JOY & THE PASTOR

Happy are those who don't stumble and fall because of me.
— Matthew 11:6 (CEB)

The Pastoral Jesus reminds us that to know blessing is to know belonging and to know belonging to be blessed. That said, whenever I see folks blast #blessed, I silently mock. Okay fine. Often, it's out loud. I cringe because too often blessing is used as a superficial mask of happiness. On the other hand, genuine joy brings life to every part of our body and soul.

We must understand blessedness not only as God's generous expression of love, but also as being part of God's cloud of witnesses, ancestors, and saints who also collectively experience belonging. A true blessing is to know that God knows each and every one of us, no matter where we are, what we have, or who we are.

To be deeply blessed on this day is to know that God loves you, loves me, loves us, and loves even those whom we cannot bring ourselves to love. To fully believe and boldly live this knowledge is indeed a blessing for which we can give thanks.

Advent Candle Lighting Litany

One: Immanuel, "God with us," as we light the candle of joy, we remember that Jesus comes into the world as a Pastor with us.

ALL: God, you enter the world and remind us that we are your gathered and in you we experience belonging. We rejoice that we are seen, known, and loved.

One: So with hearts, minds, and spirits filled with gratitude for being seen and known, we light the candle of JOY.

Light the candle of joy.

One: Joining the pastors of the past and calling the pastors of the future...

ALL:...the pastors of today together say, AMEN.

Preaching Prompt: How might we see enemies differently? Is blessing others—even an enemy who might deserve it—both a prophetic and a pastoral responsibility?

DAY 16

GENERATIONS

The God of heavenly forces proclaims: Elders will again dwell in the plazas of Jerusalem. Each of them will have a staff in their hand because of their great age. The city will be full of children playing in its plazas. — **Zechariah 8:4–5 (CEB, non-gendered)**

I desperately hope that as I age, I do not become crankier but become even more open to the possibilities that God may reveal. It has always been my intention to be wiser today than yesterday and wiser tomorrow than today. My intention is to keep that up until my time on earth is complete. We'll see how that goes.

In this culture, where our first instinct is to resist aging and romanticize youth, the Priestly Jesus invites us to understand how saints and ancestors formed us today and how we will form our descendants. We do this by more thoughtfully embracing shifting roles, sharing power, and living genuine encouragement. Through interactions with ancient and modern means, we are reminded that God is a God for all ages, and because of that our faith is that much richer.

Like my mentors, ancestors, and pioneers of the faith, no matter what God has in store, I'm here for it. Whatever possibilities may be revealed before me, I will faithfully take my place in the journey and boldly embrace the wisdom that was passed to me from generations past, and in turn I will pass it along to generations to come.

Who are the next generations of prophets, priests, pastors, and poets who you are coming alongside?

God with us –

From generation to generation

You reveal pathways before us all.

In these seasons and rhythms of life

may we all strive to listen and follow.

– AMEN

DAY 17

FINISHED

You are all God's children through faith in Christ Jesus. All of you who were baptized into Christ have clothed yourselves with Christ. — **Galatians 3:26–27 (CEB)**

As I approach the final part of life, I sometimes wish I could be done. Can I just get the keys to my island already, where I can spend all day eating mangoes, drinking boba, and floating in the ocean? Oh, and if I might avoid politics, strife, or anything that forces me to think, struggle, or grow—bonus!

Okay, I know that this existence would get old, but I also know that the Poetic Jesus would constantly be prodding to tell me "God is not done with you." Because as much as we would like to be finished, faith is about movement, growth, and never really being done. God always seems to dream more for us than we can dream for ourselves. Ugh. God.

Yes, there will be moments of respite, there may be a life stage of retirement, and there will even be some tasks that will indeed go unfinished. But, when it comes to being called by God, until our earthly time is up, I rejoice that God and I are not yet done.

What might God still have in store for you in the future?

God with us –

Faith is never finished seeking,

finished asking, or finished growing.

Instead, faith demands that we trust the

wanderings of the Spirit and follow.

– AMEN

DAY 18

SAVED

Restore us, God of heavenly forces! Make your face shine so that we can be saved! — **Psalm 80:19 (CEB, non-gendered)**

Saved is a word that gives many the shivers because it has often been used as justification for the oppression and abuse of so many in the name of Jesus Christ. Well, folks, the Prophet Jesus would like to have a word, because we have lost what it means to experience salvation in its most grace-filled form: God's intention to have each of connected to God for eternity.

Salvation is not about placing shackles on the minds, hands, and hearts of ourselves or others. Instead, it is about being liberated by choosing to believe that, for eternity, we have been reconnected to God and are called to a new way of seeing and living. This must not be a lens of rigidity and narrowing of the world, but one of discovering the expansive nature of God and the world that God has created.

Being saved is not about being shoved into a box of behavior and thought, but about being freed to build and bolster a new life in Christ. So with great joy, let us claim our salvation and live as if it matters.

What were you taught about salvation? What do you believe now? What questions do you still have?

God with us –

I revel in the unearned gift of life eternal.

Saved not from faltering or struggle

but saved from the need to judge

myself or others.

– AMEN

DAY 19

KNOWN

But now, after knowing God (or rather, being known by God), how can you turn back again to the weak and worthless world system? Do you want to be slaves to it again?
— Galatians 4:9 (CEB)

I am always moved when someone who met me only once or twice not only knows my name but also remembers something about me. Creating conditions where we are known by others is at the center of the calling of the Pastoral Jesus.

But to *know* in the ways God hopes, we must know not only the people around us but also the realities of world around us. Few things broaden our experience of God more than becoming aware of the new in the world: new perspectives, new experiences, and new possibilities. While many new experiences are positive, some are often heartbreaking: the troubling history of our own families, the suffering of communities that went go unnoticed, or global realities that we have only heard of but not really known about. Whether our new awareness is positive or negative, knowing makes it impossible to be the same in the future.

Sometimes we protect ourselves and our children from knowledge because we are afraid of how our and their lives might change. While we must be discerning as to what exposure is healthy, we must also fully embrace and pursue a breadth of knowledge—because no matter how difficult it may be to see, the fullness of creation is where God is.

The path of faith, along with mystery and experience, is strewn with the gift of knowing, so let us not miss the chance to know God and ourselves better.

What are a few new things you have learned or experienced lately?

God with us –

We didn't always know of your love:

Your deep and abiding love.

But now that we know, let us live

as if this knowledge matters.

– AMEN

DAY 20

LIFE

The Holy One! God brings death, gives life, takes down to the grave, and raises up! — **1 Samuel 2:6 (CEB, non-gendered)**

Our culture does not handle struggle, grief, or sadness well. We want people to get over it or move on too quickly. We want people to stop making us feel uncomfortable with their emotions. We ask people how they are doing without really wanting to know the depths of the despair and sadness that they may be experiencing.

One of the worst things we do in response to those experiencing grief, loss, or sorrow is to justify or soften the grief by offering some form of "This was part of God's plan" or "Think of all the blessings you have." We then expect those sad people to respond, "Oh, in that case, I'm happy now." These kinds of responses can be hurtful and even harmful to those who receive them.

The Priestly Jesus reminds us that when we are in our deepest places of struggle, while we may not always believe it at that exact moment, remembering that God is in the midst of both death *and* life will allow us to embrace what is next. God's part in all of this is simply to be present.

How has God been present in a time of grief or sorrow in the past?

God with us –

Let us trust that in our deepest places of

despair, agony, and even death,

in your time only

you will bring hope, joy, and life.

– AMEN

DAY 21

CONNECTIONS

So there were fourteen generations from Abraham to David, fourteen generations from David to the exile to Babylon, and fourteen generations from the exile to Babylon to the Christ.
— Matthew 1:17 (CEB)

As we look around the world, we may witness the rise of violence being perpetrated by someone upon a stranger, by a neighbor on a loved one, by a state on another state, and by governments on their citizens. I can't help but believe that if each person in the world felt a little more connected to the other, we would be in a better place.

It's okay for people to stand alone against injustice or boldly step into new spaces of personal growth. At the same time, the Pastoral Jesus reminds us that the strength of our individual selves is intrinsically connected to the health of the entire body. Being an individual and embracing the unique ways in which we are created by God is vital. At the same time, we must remember that our individual choices impact others. They must not come at the cost of the community's life, agency, and dignity or those connected to us.

This journey of faith, both shared and solo, is rarely for us and us alone, so the more we remember that others walk with us, the more likely we all are to live into the possibilities that God intends for us all.

Thinking about communities that you are currently a part of, where do you see the most collaboration, and where do you see the most division?

God with us –

Whether by cells or circumstance,

we are inextricably connected.

Let us receive this not as a burden to bear

but as a gift to nurture.

- AMEN

The Fourth Sunday in Advent

DAY 22: THE FOURTH SUNDAY IN ADVENT

LOVE & THE POET

Nothing is impossible for God. — **Luke 1:37 (CEB)**

I do not want to love my enemy. My enemies have hurt me; they have inflicted violence upon communities that I care about; they have legislated systems of exclusion; and they have reinforced systems of oppression. My enemies have made my heart hate.

And yet we know that even our enemies are worthy of God's love.

The Poet Jesus constantly shows love for the marginalized *and* for those who hold power in systems of marginalization. In doing so, he shows that loving our enemy is not only a possibility but a reality. The Poet Jesus challenges us to stretch our hearts wider than we would do ourselves, not to put ourselves in harm's way or to allow ourselves to be taken advantage of, but to live boldly the truth that all of God's created are loved.

Advent Candle Lighting Litany

One: Immanuel, "God with us," as we light the candle of love, we remember that Jesus comes into the world as a Poet with us.

ALL: God, you enter the world and challenge us to dream about what could be for our lives, the lives of others, and the life of the world.

One: So it is with this foolishness and audacity that we open ourselves up to God's unexpected hopes and intentions for humanity and the world, that we light the candle of LOVE.
Light the candle of love.

One: Joining the poets of the past and calling the poets of the future...

ALL:...the poets of today together say, AMEN.

Preaching Prompt: In what places and situations does loving our enemy seem the most out of reach? How might we show and/or receive unconditional love? Help your people get there and paint a picture of what that love might look like there.

DAY 23

MINDFUL

Mary said, "With all my heart I glorify God! In the depths of who I am I rejoice in God my savior. God has looked with favor on the low status of their servant. Look! From now on, everyone will consider me highly favored."
— Luke 1:46–48 (CEB, non-gendered)

I am the *worst* at remembering to send birthday notes to my family. I have tons of excuses: I'm too busy; they don't mind; I am just bad at this. While all are true and real, my forgetting and the reasons I forget should not be excuses to stop trying. Being remembered is wonderful because we are reminded that we are not alone, so I should keep trying.

Under the weight of the overwhelming social and political turmoil of the day, it is all too easy to forget. We forget our loved ones, forget the struggles of the world, and forget that people live lives drastically different from ours. The Pastoral Jesus calls us to remember others and the lives they lead because in doing so we strengthen personal relationships, step out of places of privilege, and develop a deeper appreciation for the world and the people in it.

For the good of the world and our own faith, we must remember others as God remembers us.

How could you be better about remembering other people?

God with us –

When the world has us feeling

forgotten, forsaken, and overwhelmed,

speak so that we may

trust and believe

that we are always remembered by you.

– AMEN

DAY 24

ALONE

My tears have been my food both day and night, as people constantly questioned me, "Where's your God now?"
— Psalm 42:3 (CEB)

While many times in church we say, "God is with you," I know that it is often difficult for people to believe in the presence of God. If anyone was to look at the state of the world and not wonder where God is in all of this, I would be surprised. Because sometimes it does feel as if God has walked away. When I am feeling apart from God, simply telling me to stop feeling this way does not work. In fact, it may make me feel even worse.

To believe that God is near is an act of faithful choosing. The Priestly Jesus invites us into ritual and discipline intended to support our open connection to God. Being open to the possibility to trust that God is present even when we are not feeling it is the first step. It is natural to sometimes feel apart from or abandoned by God. We will feel lost, angry, and ignored. This is okay. God can handle it. But just as we hope that others will get a glimpse of God through our words and actions, we too must remain open to the ways in which God is made known to us.

Where do you feel apart from God? Where is God most present?

God with us –

When I feel alone, isolated,

and abandoned by You,

give me the fortitude and faith

to hear the whispers reminding me

that you never left.

- AMEN

DAY 25

BORDERS

But when it saw ahead of time that God would make the Gentiles righteous on the basis of faith, scripture preached the gospel in advance to Abraham: All the Gentiles will be blessed in you. — **Galatians 3:8 (CEB)**

God does not have citizenship in any country. That might not be obvious, given the hyper-patriotic rhetoric and xenophobia that have infested so much Christian messaging and nationalized cruelty today. At this phenomenon, I believe God weeps.

As the reverberations of "God Bless America" continue to guide so many U.S. Christians, I believe that the Prophet Jesus would want to disrupt the idea of borders and nation-states altogether and challenge us to see people of all lands as blessed by God. What if we believe that God blesses not only the United States, but also China, Chile, Greenland, North Korea, Jamaica, Nigeria, the Philippines, Venezuela, Russia, South Korea, Iraq, Israel, Ukraine, Haiti, Azerbaijan, Cameroon, Tonga, Palestine, Syria, Ethiopia, Fiji, and every other country in the world? In doing so, we would soon realize the concept of God's nation and how each citizen cares for its members is far different than modern-day nation-states and the borders that humans have drawn, militarized, and controlled.

As we ask for blessings upon our own country, let us expand the borders of belief around who else God blesses.

Do you believe God blesses people in one country more than people in another?

God with us –

You are beyond the borders and bounds

that nations have placed upon creation.

In response to steadfast, hateful separation,

let us choose committed, holy collaboration.

– AMEN

CHRISTMAS EVE

WELCOME

> *While they were there, the time came for Mary to have her baby. She gave birth to her firstborn child, a son, wrapped him snugly, and laid him in a manger, because there was no place for them in the guestroom.* — **Luke 2:6–7 (CEB)**

For years, like many I too heard the Christmas story with some version of "Jesus was born into the messiness of the world after his family was rejected by the ones he came to love." Then I took a trip to Palestine, and my world got shook.

During a stop in one of the oldest Christian villages in the world, we were given a tour of what a home would have looked like in the time of Jesus. During that time, the animals did not live in a separate space as we would assume today. They shared the same space; in fact, the animals were kept warm and cared for as they helped provide life for the family. We also were shown that deeply rooted in Palestinian culture, then as today, is a commitment to radical hospitality and welcoming the stranger. This means that when Mary and Joseph found themselves without a place to lay their heads, they were undoubtedly welcomed into someone's home for the night.

In this, the fourfold nature of Jesus completes the journey: The Prophetic Jesus tells of God's intentions that we too should welcome the stranger with hospitality; the Priestly Jesus challenges to keep reexamining the narratives that we tell ourselves; the Pastoral Jesus invites us to expand the idea of who makes up the household of God; and the Poetic Jesus inspires us to believe that goodness does not always have to be born of strife, but can also be born from goodness itself.

Merry Christmas!

When have you been unexpectedly invited into someone's home and shown radical hospitality?

God with us –

Born into chaos and fear

Born into hospitality and welcome

With the arrival of the Christ child

Let us know the fullness of your welcome with hope, peace, joy and love.

– AMEN

CHRISTMAS DAY

REJOICE

Suddenly a great assembly of the heavenly forces was with the angel praising God. They said, "Glory to God in heaven, and on earth peace among those whom God favors."
— Luke 2:13–14 (CEB, non-gendered)

As a pastor, I *love it* when Christmas falls on a Sunday. Because of the chaos of the season, we can play a bit, and play we do. My go-to service was always "Doughnuts, Pajamas, and Carols," not necessarily in that order but usually simultaneously. We gathered as we were, we ate donuts, and we sang Christmas carols with all the gusto each deserves.

Sometimes Christians can be *soooo* serious. We often hold back for fear of being too emotional, "extra," or arrogant about faith. Depending on the context, these may be good instincts. But sometimes, in body, mind, and spirit, we need to rejoice boldly, for when done faithfully, the world can tell the difference.

On this day, as we celebrate the birth of Christ with all the disruption, grounding, belonging, and imagination he brings to the world, let us also remember that this is an event fully deserving of our souls' most joyful noise. So as we welcome and celebrate the birth of the Christ child, let our bodies, minds, hearts, and souls rejoice and be glad in it!

It will be okay. God will not get mad.

What are some of your fondest Christmas memories?

God with us –

Yes, we told it from the mountain.

We welcomed, we received, and we rejoiced.

Let today's elation not fade away,

but embolden us for tomorrow.

– AMEN

THE DAY AFTER

GAZE

Because they were warned in a dream not to return to Herod, they went back to their own country by another route.
— Matthew 2:12 (CEB)

Pardon me as I end Advent devotions with a story about Pentecost, which reminds me of Epiphany and makes a ton of sense for the day after Christmas.

I have a friend in Palestine who often shares that his family converted to Christianity at *the* Pentecost. Not during a Pentecost service sometime in the past, but at *the* first one. He tells the story to remind people that hope and God's revealing of God's intentions do not always follow the timeline we may wish for overcoming the suffering of the world. Overcoming the gluttony of empire and the evils of the day may take generations. My friend shares this insight not as a downer, but as a word of hope: Love will outlast hate.

He also shares that we now have a role in manifesting the "kin-dom," and that may involve taking an unexpected, even risky path, just as the Magi did. This is so that Jesus who comes into the world may be known. We learn to gaze into the future of what is promised while staring down the path of possibilities before us, knowing that we do so with the Prophet, Priest, Pastor, and Poet Jesus by our side along the way.

How will you live differently as the season turns? What gives you hope? What concerns you?

God with us –

Yesterday, today, and tomorrow.

We look forward, we look ahead, we look down.

Let us see the possibilities in you

so we may work toward the possibilities for all.

– AMEN

The Last Word

AI Disclaimers

Google spell check was used to offer spelling correction suggestions, and Grammarly was used to offer clarity suggestions, but never for content. No question was ever asked of ChatGPT, Claude, Gemini, or any other AI platform to help in the formation or content building while writing this book. The idea that "the future is now" has never felt so true.

Stay in Touch

Email: bruce@reyes-chow.com

Website and *The Amalgamation* Newsletter: www.reyes-chow.com

The Amalgamation Podcast: bit.ly/AmalgamationPod

Social media platforms via @breyeschow

Book Groups

If your book group uses this or any of my previous books, as I am able, I would love to join your group via video call for a discussion (free). To arrange book group meetings and for all other speaking inquiries, please reach out to: theteam@reyes-chow.com.

Book Discount

If your group would like to purchase any of my books published by Chalice Media, please be sure to visit ChalicePress.com for bulk discounts.

Rediscover Jesus. Reimagine Faith.

A powerful new book and two seasonal devotionals from Bruce Reyes-Chow invite you to encounter Christ as prophet, priest, pastor, and poet—and become part of God's transforming work in the world.

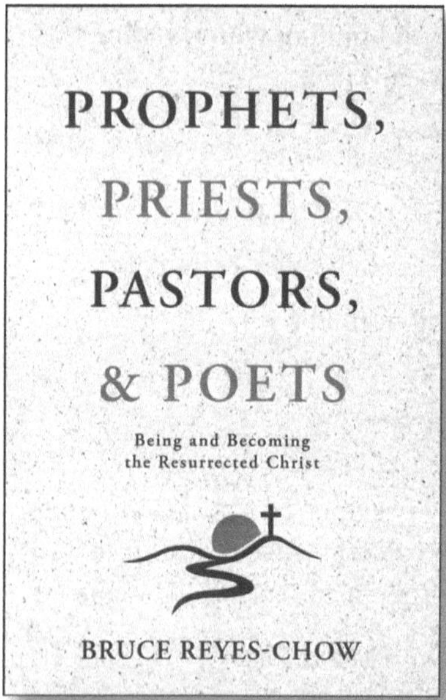

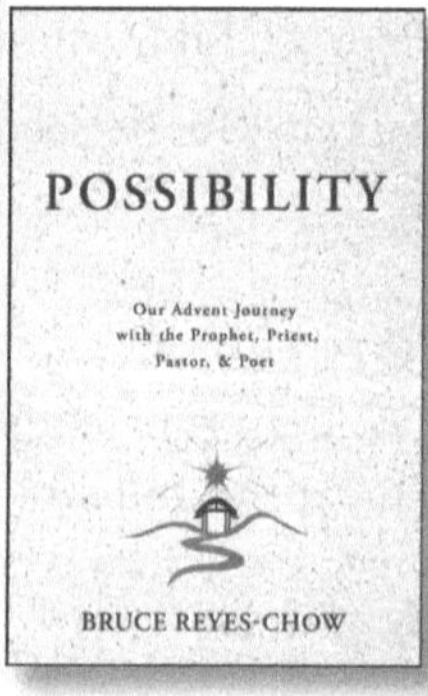

Prophets, Priests, Pastors, & Poets *(Available September 2026)*
Being and Becoming the Resurrected Christ
9780827231948

Possibility *(Available September 2026)*
Our Advent Journey with the Prophet, Priest, Pastor, & Poet
9780827231979

Beckon *(Available December 2026)*
Our Lent Journey with the Prophet, Priest, Pastor, & Poet
9780827203471

chalice PRESS

Available at ChalicePress.com
and wherever you buy books

Also Available from Bruce Reyes-Chow

"A simple, yet staggering work that examines a precious and rare commodity in this present world."
—*Jeff Yang, CNN & Wall Street Journal*

In Defense of Kindness

Why It Matters, How It Changes Our Lives,
and How It Can Save the World

9780827216761

chalice PRESS

Available at ChalicePress.com
and wherever you buy books